Books by Sam Polson

In His Image

*By Faith: Timeless Insights for Staying on
Course from Hebrews 11*

*SonLight: Daily Light from the
Pages of God's Word*

*Corona Victus:
Conquering the Virus of Fear*

Life Changing Prayer

LIFE CHANGING PRAYER

Sam Polson

[handwritten inscription]

2 Cor. 4:5

4/15/21

To Terrie,
My friend and sister
in Lord. May you
experience Life Changing
Prayer! God Bless!
Sam Polson

Angel Climbing Publishing

Life Changing Prayer
Written by Sam Polson

Transcribed and edited by Lisa Soland

Published in 2020 by:
Climbing Angel Publishing
PO Box 32381
Knoxville, Tennessee 37930
http://www.ClimbingAngel.com

First Edition: December 2020
Printed in the United States of America
Cover design by PrintEdge
Author photo by Stefan Holt
Interior design by Climbing Angel Publishing

ISBN: 978-1-64921-785-1
Library of Congress Control Number: 2020922500

To Susan,
My Beloved Prayer Partner
"Always & Forever"

Contents

Introduction

WHEN I WAS ABOUT EIGHT YEARS OLD, MY older brother Lonny joined the Boy Scouts. In addition to the uniform, he was required to purchase all sorts of interesting equipment.

And of course, being an eight-year-old boy, I was very curious about what my brother was doing. So, when he was out of our room, I often got into his stuff.

Among his Boy Scout "tools-of-the-trade," I discovered the neatest thing—a magnifying glass. It closed up into a little red pouch that had the scout emblem on it. Believe it or not, my brother wasn't nearly as interested in the magnifying glass as I was. A few years later, he gave it to me, and yes, I still have it to this day.

As a young boy, I carried the magnifying glass in my pocket. I loved looking for opportunities to use it whenever I could. Then one day, as I was playing with it outside, examining a single leaf very closely, I stumbled upon something exciting. I could set things on fire with that piece of glass! I had no idea what was going on. I did not understand the science behind it, but I was having the time of my life.

I would gather a handful of leaves, situate them in the sunshine, and focus that beam of light onto the pile. The next thing you knew, a little fire would begin. On one occasion, a couple of big ants strolled by, and I thought to myself, *I wonder if this glass will do to ants what it does to leaves?* Well, sure enough, it did just about the same thing. Those ants became *fire ants,* but I was the one creating the fire!

I also noticed that sometimes when I used that magnifying glass, a rainbow would appear. And as I got a bit older, in one of my science classes at school, I learned that the magnifying glass is actually a *prism* that bends the light's path. The path of that light is actually made up of wavelengths of light that you normally cannot see, but when they are bent, you can see the various spectral colors of that beam of light, and the result is a beautiful rainbow.

I use this story as an illustration because when you think of light, you really don't *see* light. You see how light illuminates things. But when you take those rays of light and bend them, you can see and experience this beautiful rainbow of colors.

What a *prism* does to light, prayer does for our relationship with God. There are things we can only see about God through *spiritual eyesight.* Through prayer, the invisible God becomes *visible* to our souls as we experience incredible and infinite expressions of His glory. By focusing on God through different *lenses* of prayer, we are able to *see* Him, *know* Him, and *experience* Him in beautiful varieties of his ever-amazing grace and love.

In this book, *Life Changing Prayer*, we will be using the word "*prism*" as an acrostic to guide us in our approach of time with God so that, through various types of prayer, we will begin to *see* and *experience* different aspects of Him. Our acrostic P.R.I.S.M. includes prayers of *Praise,* prayers of *Repentance,* prayers of *Intercession,* prayers of *Specific Requests,* and prayers of *Meditation.*

It is my sincere prayer that this small volume will encourage and increase the devotional times of many believers. May it serve as a guiding light to experience the beauty of our God as He changes your life through prayer.

Sam Polson
November 2020

PRAISE
R
I
S
M

1

THERE IS JUST SOMETHING BREATHTAKING about a rainbow. It captures our attention and captivates our souls, perhaps as nothing else. In fact, a rainbow so touches our hearts that we are compelled to call its attention to others or snap pictures to share with our friends. Recently, when I was on a trip away from home, a beautiful rainbow appeared in our community. Within a few minutes, my phone was literally blowing up with people sending me their pictures of the amazing site.

All the colors of the rainbow, that beautiful *prism* of light, touch us and move us in the most profound ways. Something of such beauty must be praised. The wonder of prayer begins here, with the praise of the Most Perfectly Beautiful of all—the glorious God who causes all things to exist. He simply must be praised. No greater privilege can be experienced or expressed than to offer praise to the One whose throne is encircled by the heavenly rainbow.

Praise is central to the ultimate purpose of all life, and therefore, praise needs to be at the very center of our regular prayer life. In this chapter, we want to focus on the ultimate priority of praise while we pray.

First and foremost, we should praise God because...

GOD IS WORTHY OF PRAISE

Praise is the very atmosphere of heaven. There are passages in the *Book of the Revelation* where the curtain of time is pulled back, and we are allowed to look into glory and see what is happening in the eternal presence of God. As we do, we learn that praise is the *language* of heaven. God is praised by the inhabitants of heaven for *Who* He is.

> And the four living creatures, each of them with six wings, are full of eyes all around and within, and day and night they never cease to say, "Holy, holy, holy, is the Lord God Almighty, who was and is and is to come!" And whenever the living creatures give glory and honor and thanks to him who is seated on the throne, who lives forever and ever, the twenty-four elders [the redeemed] fall down before

him who is seated on the throne and worship him who lives forever and ever. They cast their crowns before the throne, saying, "Worthy are you, our Lord and God, to receive glory and honor and power, for you created all things, and by your will they existed and were created."

(Revelation 4:8-11)

Praise is rising continually from the holy angels and the holy people of God whose spirits are present with the Lord. Angels and saints praise God for who He is. He is God. He is the great Creator. He is worthy. God is praised first and foremost for who He is.

God is also praised *for what He has done.* In fact, there is praise offered in heaven into which the angels cannot participate because they have never experienced what that praise celebrates. The saints in heaven praise God (and we should join with them here on Earth) for what He has done in saving our souls and redeeming our lives from destruction.

> And they sang a new song, saying, "Worthy are you to take the scroll and to open its seals, for you were slain, and by your blood you ransomed people for God from every tribe and language and people and nation, and you have made them a

> kingdom and priests to our God, and
> they shall reign on the earth."
> (Revelation 5:9-10)

This is praise that no angel can offer because they lack the personal experience. No angel has ever experienced the joy of sins forgiven, the freedom of redemption, or the astounding reality of adoption as a child of God through Jesus Christ. They must fold their wings and listen in wonder as believers exult in God's salvation. Every Christian can praise the Lord for *Who He is* and for *what He has done*.

How often is God the sole focus of our prayers? How often do we pray and *not ask* God for anything? How often do we simply glory in who He is or praise Him for what He has done? Praising God in prayer is so powerful. As Christians, every day is a day to praise the Lord. No matter what is happening in our lives, we are His, and He is ours forever and ever. And that is surely something to praise Him about!

So why should we praise God? Because He is worthy of it and also *because we were saved to praise the Lord*.

WE WERE SAVED TO PRAISE GOD

In the 4th Chapter of John's gospel, we are told about an occasion when Jesus and his disciples traveled through Samaria. The disciples certainly did not want to take this detour from the customary route, but Jesus was compelled in His spirit to go where Jewish people rarely ventured. The Jews were not welcome in Samaria, but Jesus placed it on His travel itinerary because He had a very important noon appointment with a lady at the village well to discuss the water supply. She didn't know she had the appointment with Him, but Jesus already had it on both their calendars.

This woman's life was as empty as her water jar. She had known abuse by men all of her adult life. She came to the well with a life that was parched, joyless, and hopeless. She cannot visit the well in the morning when the ladies from the city regularly come to fill their water jars and "fill up" on local news. She knows by personal experience that they won't accept her because of her past life and her present reputation. So, she must visit the well in solitude and in the heat of the day.

Arriving at the well, she is no doubt shocked to discover a Jewish rabbi sitting there and is even more amazed when a few moments later, he actually asks her for a drink of water. This is startling because it is unheard of that a Jewish man, especially a Rabbi, would ask her, a Samaritan woman, for a drink of water. He has definitely captured her attention.

In reply to her question, Jesus begins to share with this woman (the least likely recipient imaginable) the greatest truths concerning the nature of God and the focus of His worldwide mission. The woman very quickly becomes uncomfortable with the extent of knowledge this mysterious rabbi has about her life, so she tries to change the topic of conversation by arguing religion. Jesus interrupts her attempts at deflection, saying,

> But the hour is coming, and is now here, when the true worshipers will worship the Father in spirit and truth, for the Father is seeking such people to worship him. (John 4:23)

Note that "spirit and truth." The worship that is done "*in spirit and truth*" means worship that expresses all of a person's heart, responding to all that God is.

Jesus continues His revelation about worship, saying, "...the Father is seeking such people to worship him." Here we learn the heart of God's mission—seeking worshipers. Notice God is the Seeker. The truth is none of us were, in reality, seeking God. If God had not actively pursued us, we would never have sought Him. By nature, we are rebel sinners, running as fast away from God as we can, but God in His grace seeks us. His goal in seeking us is to make Himself known so that we can worship Him in *spirit and in truth.*

This does not mean that God is selfish or needy. God doesn't need anything. He is completely sufficient in Himself. So when Jesus says that the Father desires to be worshiped, it's not because He is in need of something. The Father desires our worship because of what He can give us through that worship. God gives the greatest of all gifts to worshipers—*the gift of Himself.*

God created us so that we might *know Him* and *enjoy Him*. It is through Christ alone that we are able to be brought back into a personal relationship with God for which we were created, a relationship of knowing Him and enjoying Him. This is what worshipers do. We are saved for the purpose of worship, and a very significant aspect of this worship is *praising God.*

In Ephesians 1:1-15, Paul reminds us several times regarding the purpose of our salvation by declaring we were saved for the "praise of His glory." Meaning, we were not saved for our glory but for the praise of *His* glory.

> ...who is the guarantee of our inheritance until we acquire possession of it, **to the praise of his glory**. For this reason, because I

have heard of your faith in the Lord
Jesus and your love toward all the
saints, (Ephesians 1:14-15)

So, if we truly want to experience the
"purpose-driven life," we must live the
"purpose-fueled life," fueled by praise. We were
saved to be worshipers. When we worship God
in praise, we are fulfilling our purpose. Perhaps
like me, you have noticed that when you are
praising God, you never feel more complete or
more whole because this is exactly why God
saved us. He has saved you and me to praise
Him.

So why should we praise God when we
pray? Because He's worthy of it, because we
were saved to do it, and because *Jesus taught
us to do it*.

JESUS TAUGHT US TO PRAISE GOD

Now Jesus was praying in a certain
place, and when he finished, one of
his disciples said to him, "Lord,
teach us to pray, as John taught his
disciples." And he said to them,
"When you pray, say: "Father,
hallowed be your name. Your
kingdom come." (Luke 11:1-2)

The disciples had carefully observed how
their Master prayed, and they deeply desired

Jesus to teach them how to pray just like He did. This is not to say that they never prayed, but they didn't pray like Jesus prayed. His prayers were not the typical, memorized recitations of archaic words so common to the religious leaders of the day. No, the prayers of Jesus were so personal, so intimate, so real. They wanted to pray like that. So Jesus shared with them a *model prayer*.

It is not really "The *Lord's* Prayer" because there are things in this prayer that Jesus could never pray. Jesus could not pray, "Forgive us this day our debts as we forgive our debtors," because Jesus had no spiritual debts or transgressions. Instead, Jesus is teaching the disciples a prayer pattern that *they* can follow, so it is really "The Disciple's Prayer." Jesus told them, "When you pray, say: 'Father, hallowed [holy] be your name. Your kingdom come...'" (Luke 11:1-2).

The first thing Jesus taught His disciples about prayer was to make their prayers God-focused—"*Your*" name be praised, "*Your*" kingdom come, "*Your*" will be done. That language is *God-exalting* language and *God-focused* language. Jesus is instructing His disciples, back then and through the ages, that the first priority in prayer is praise.

The first focus of prayer is not "to ask." Of course, there is certainly nothing wrong with asking in very specific ways (as we will discuss in a later chapter), but praise is to be paramount in prayer.

Praising God in prayer is our first priority because praise addresses our biggest problem. Our number one problem is that we are proud people. By our very nature, we are self-focused, and the greatest antidote for selfishness is praise. In fact, praise poisons pride.

As a young boy, I discovered my dad had the neatest tool in our backyard shed—a hand-pump sprayer. I used to watch my dad going around the garden, pumping that sprayer, and I thought, *That is the greatest thing!*

One evening, I decided to try out the sprayer, so I walked along our wire fence, pumping and pumping the sprayer until it was completely empty. Of course, I was oblivious to where the wind was carrying that spray.

My home town was nicknamed "Rose City" because of the beautiful roses that were grown there and our next-door neighbor, Miss Margeson, grew some of the most prized roses every year. She was also *extremely proud* of her roses. Now, those roses just happened to be growing directly on the other side of that fence, where I had been spraying away!

A few days later, I heard Miss Margeson telling my mother, with a broken voice, that something had killed her prized roses. While she shared this information with my mother, I quickly found something else to be doing and conveniently disappeared! After many, many years, I am finally confessing via this book on prayer!

However, I did learn several lessons from that experience, one of them being that those flowers of pride were no match for my father's poison! In a very real way, all of our lives are fertile soil for the flowers of pride. Fortunately, our Heavenly Father has a poison for the pride that blooms in our hearts—*Praise. Praise poisons pride.*

The opposite of pride is humility. What produces the beautiful flower of humility? Humility is brought about by being in the presence of someone *really* great. We often think that we are something special until we are in the presence of someone *truly* great.

The only true and ultimately great person in the universe is God Himself. Only God is great. People who consistently come before God, spending time in praise, will naturally bow their heads in humility because they are in the presence of the Great and Holy One. His presence and our praise poisons pride.

So, why should we include praise in our prayer time? Because God is worthy of it, we were saved to do it, Jesus taught us to do it, and fourthly, because Satan hates it.

SATAN HATES IT

Our world suffers from a lot of pollution, and much of it is *noise pollution*. I hear it regularly driving up and down a main thoroughfare in Knoxville, Tennessee, where I live. People in tiny little cars want to make their vehicles sound like really big race cars. They rev up their engines, intending to make them sound much larger than they are. Frankly, it drives me to distraction and my wife to laughing at my response!

Noise pollution is a problem, and it is often a problem in our thought life. Satan, the god of this world, pollutes this world with a lot of corrupt noise—the noise of lies, the noise of filth, and the noise of things completely contrary to God's truth. Satan pollutes the air in which we live, and we must determine to battle this and "clear the air" in our minds on a daily basis. This battle against the world's "noise pollution" is an expression of *spiritual warfare*.

So how do we win in this terrible, relentless battle? The best *defense* in spiritual warfare is a good *offense*, and the most wonderful offense that we can have against the devil is praising the Lord. The devil hates the praise of God and has no defense against it. Satan hates praise, and he hates to be reminded that the Lord has won the victory over him. Most of all, he hates to hear the Name of the One who has conquered him and his kingdom—the name of Jesus Christ. This is why we need to be constantly practicing praise because it is an incredibly effective way of coming against our enemy

When we praise God, we proclaim the victory Jesus accomplished by His sacrifice on the cross. Thank God, the victory was accomplished as Jesus cried out, "It is finished!" Jesus won the victory over sin, death, and Satan, and by praising Him in prayer, we are proclaiming that victory. With our proclamations of praise, we renounce the enemy. In effect, as we *pray to God, we pray at the devil.*

Of course, the devil will not take your praise assault lightly. He will remind you of all the things you have done wrong. But remember this counter-measure—when the devil *reminds you of your past, remind him of his future.* His future is not so hot. Well, actually, that's not true. Satan's future is going to be very, very hot forever!

For a Christian, praise is how we pledge allegiance. Praise is how we pledge allegiance to our King by taking a knee for Him. Take a knee before the Lord. Even better, take *both* knees. Simply get on your knees and praise the Lord, your Captain and King. Praise Him. And let the devil listen to your "praise of allegiance."

This warfare tactic of praise was displayed over 2700 years ago in the days of King Jehoshaphat, King of Judah. The land was surrounded by a massive army of countless legions coming to destroy the nation and murder and enslave the people. Jehoshaphat prayed fervently to Jehovah, "Lord, we do not know what to do but our eyes are on you." That is a great prayer! That is a prayer of desperation and dependence. God answered, commanding the armies to go forward and to trust in Him. We are told how King Jehoshaphat organized the army around praise to advance against this dreadful foe:

> And they rose early in the morning and went out into the wilderness of Tekoa. And when they went out, Jehoshaphat stood and said, "Hear me, Judah and inhabitants of Jerusalem! Believe in the Lord your God, and you will be established; believe his prophets, and you will succeed." And when he had taken counsel with the people, he appointed those who were to sing to the Lord and praise him in holy attire, as they went before the army, and say, "Give thanks to the Lord, for his steadfast love endures forever." (2 Chronicles 20:20-21)

Notice, not elite soldiers, but people praising the name of the Lord God led Judah's armies. What should we learn from this account about spiritual warfare? We need to recognize that in spiritual warfare, there is tremendous power in the praise of God. "There is none like you, O Lord; you are great, and your name is great in might" (Jer. 10:6).

We need to let Satan know whose side we are on. Make sure he knows whose colors you are wearing. Let him know who your Captain is. You may not be the best representative for the team, but remind the devil who your team Captain and Head Coach are. We are wearing the salvation garments of the Lord Jesus Christ. Remind the devil whose side you are on; declare it out loud. "I belong to the team of Jesus Christ!"

Lastly, we need to praise God, not only because Satan hates it, Jesus said to do it, we were saved to do it, He is worthy of it, but also *because the world needs it.*

THE WORLD NEEDS IT

Our mission is for the renown of the Lord's name, and we are commissioned to be a part of making His name known. In 1 Chronicles 16, we are given the account of David bringing the ark back to Mount Zion, the place where the tabernacle was erected in Jerusalem. Jerusalem was now the capital of the twelve united tribes of Israel.

As the tribes were uniting into one nation, David did not want them united around him, but rather around the God of Israel. So, David and a huge crowd of the people of Israel brought the ark to Mount Zion in a celebration of praise and worship. The hills and valleys surrounding Jerusalem resounded with praise:

> Sing to the Lord, all the earth! Tell of his salvation from day to day. Declare his glory among the nations, his marvelous works among all the peoples!
> (1 Chronicles 16:23-24)

The Lord wants the testimony of His renown and the glory of His Name to be proclaimed to all the people groups throughout *the world,* and we are the messengers.

So, where does "the world" begin for you? It may very well begin in your neighborhood. It may begin in your classroom. It may begin in the area surrounding your cubical at your office. "The world" may begin today at a sporting event or some other gathering your scheduled to attend. But wherever you are, that is where your world begins, and that is most certainly a place that needs to hear the praise of the Lord. Be prepared, wherever you are, to give praise to God.

Our mission begins in private, but it must not stay private. We need to practice in private what we are going to proclaim in public. Before we ever talk about Jesus *publicly*, we need to be sure that we are talking to Jesus *privately*. This is so important to remember. God wants us to proclaim His name in private *and* in public.

Our world needs our Lord. The Lord is the answer. He is the answer to *every need*. We who have come to know this wonderful reality and provision in Jesus have the privilege and responsibility to make Him known by sharing His praise.

Praise is our continual sacrifice. We no longer follow the sacrificial system of the Old Covenant because Christ has, once and for all, put away sin. He is the Lamb of God who takes away the sin of the world. However, you and I, as Christians, still have sacrifices to offer. We must offer *ourselves* to the Lord. "Present your bodies as a living sacrifice, holy and acceptable to God" (Rom. 12:1). This is our reasonable service we are told to perform. We also have another sacrifice to offer continually to our God according to God's Word:

> Through him then let us continually
> offer up a sacrifice of praise to God,

that is, the fruit of lips that
acknowledge his name.
(Hebrews 13:15)

The continuing "burnt offering" is our
praise to the Lamb, who became the burnt
offering on the cross but is now alive
forevermore. To the Living Lamb, we offer the
continual sacrifice, that is, the praise from our
lips as we give thanks to His holy Name.

Now, brothers and sisters, having seen the
beautiful light of praise again, determine to
dwell in this light and share this light
everywhere. Take some time right now and
warm your soul in the light of His praise. And
then rise and carry that light of God's praise
into the shadowlands of this present world.

PRAISE

Search me, O God, and know my heart!
Try me and know my thoughts!
And see if there be any grievous way in me,
and lead me in the way everlasting!
(Psalm 139:23-24)

BEFORE OUR FAMILY HAD A VEHICLE WITH A Global Positioning System, we had an earlier form of GPS device that we used on our trips. These positioning devices have made amazing advances in sophistication over the years. However, the first GPS used by our family was only *fairly* accurate with its directions. One of our children named the beautiful feminine voice of our GPS, "Edna." I'm not sure why. Edna was usually very helpful, but sometimes, not so much. Eventually, we came up with an accurate way of describing her effectiveness, "Edna gets you close."

Because Edna had no way of being updated, we would have to be careful when passing through a city that had recently constructed new overpasses or exits. Edna would just "get you close." Sometimes she might even "get you lost!" Now we use factory-installed devices or our smartphones to stay much better positioned when traveling. But even the most up-to-date technology sometimes can fail in the guidance it provides.

How grateful we should be that we possess an infallible GPS—*God's Positioning System*! His is the ultimate GPS because wherever God says we are, that is where we are, and His GPS is never mistaken. Even better, it is not only infallible; it's also *intelligible*.

My son enjoyed changing the languages on our first GPS device...of course, without telling his mom or dad. Right about the time we needed her help with directions, Edna would start speaking in Mandarin or some other language. That was not helpful. When God wants to give us directions, He speaks with real clarity and in a manner that we can understand. We always know exactly what He's saying. Isn't that good news in today's ever-changing world?

Perhaps you have experienced carefully trying to follow your GPS only to hear it sweetly say something like this, "At your closest opportunity, make a U-turn." That is a pleasant way of saying, "Boy, are you ever going the wrong way!" It is not what we want to hear, but we need to listen if we're going to reach our destination. We especially need to listen when the voice of the Lord's spiritual GPS tells us to change direction. This is precisely what God is doing when He calls us to *repentance*. I like to refer to repentance as "God's You-Turn." When God tells us we need to change direction, it is always in our best interest to do so immediately because our Heavenly Friend wants us to be on the right road. Only His road is the way of blessing.

In Psalm 139, King David praises the Lord for His guidance through His omnipotence, His omnipresence, and His omniscience. David rejoices in declaring that God fully knew about him before he was born and would guide him to the very last day of his life. From the moment of conception to his final breath on Earth, David knew God's hand was upon him. Listen to David's praise:

> Search me, O God, and know my heart! Try me and know my thoughts! And see if there be any grievous way in me, and lead me in the way everlasting!
>
> (Psalm 139:23-24)

When David says, "And see if there be any grievous way in me," he doesn't mean that God is not already aware of what is in David's heart. What David is saying is, "God, you show me. *Reveal to me* if there is any wrong way in my life so that you can lead me onto the right path and into the way everlasting."

God's You-Turn takes place when we invite the Lord to turn the searchlight on in our hearts, and reveal to us any direction we are traveling that is unpleasing to Him. Knowing *God's way* enables us to change our direction and realign ourselves onto that path—the path that will be the way everlasting.

God's You-Turn is what repentance is all about. We agree that God's directions are right, and ours are not. We invite God to give us clear direction. When we pray in repentance to God, we are genuinely asking God to do something priceless in our hearts. God's way is always going to be the best way.

REPENTANCE MUST BE TREASURED

To better understand *prayers of repentance* and how to apply them to our prayer life, we must remember that repentance must be *treasured*. Humanly, when we speak of repentance being *treasured*, it may seem like a contradiction in terms, like treasuring a toothache because we are so prone to think of repentance as "penance." Penance is a painful price to be paid for wrongdoing, but repentance is a priceless treasure because, in reality, repentance is an invitation from God.

When we sense that God is showing us that we need to change direction and go another way, that is God's invitation for us to go with Him. It is an invitation to join the Lord and to walk with Him in fellowship. Jesus Himself proclaimed repentance and declared it to be an invitation from God.

> From that time Jesus began to preach, saying, "Repent, for the kingdom of heaven is at hand." (Matthew 4:17)

"The Kingdom of heaven is at hand" is an invitation to experience the King—an opportunity to know and follow Him.

Jesus made it clear that if we are going to experience the Kingdom, we have got to change direction. Jesus offers an invitation, and the invitation is to walk with Him. What could possibly be greater than walking through our daily life and experiencing the reality of the Lord *in* our life? What an incredible gift! This gift, however, is only enjoyed by those who are walking in the same direction as the Lord. Jesus said, "Follow me." He didn't say, "Hey, where are you going? I'll come along with you."

No, His message to us is, "You follow Me and I will show you the Kingdom of God. I will show you the incredible life-journey of experiencing God." Yes, repentance should be treasured because it is an invitation to experience God.

Repentance is also a priceless invitation because of what it means. The word for repentance in Greek is metánoia, meaning "a change of mind." It is a change of mind that leads to a change of direction. However, this change of direction doesn't start with our feet; it starts in our minds. When God calls us to repent, He is saying, "Change your mind. Turn around. Come this way. I'm inviting you." It is a message of hope because being called to repentance means that God has not given up on you. You are not a hopeless case. If God had given up on you, He wouldn't challenge you about the path you are traveling.

We are all wise enough to know that when someone loves us, they love us enough to say, "You're going the wrong way." That is a true friend. When we sense that the Lord is telling us to change our way and our direction, we must praise God for that because it means that God is interested and concerned for us. He knows what's best for us. He hasn't left us to our own devices. The cruelest thing that can ever happen to someone is to be left to their own way because those paths, by nature, are paths of destruction. They are not the paths of life.

What a joy to be able to say, "Lord, lead me in the way everlasting. Show me where I need to turn, and by Your grace, I will turn." Hebrews 12:7 reminds us,

> It is for discipline that you have to
> endure. God is treating you as sons.
> For what son is there whom his
> father does not discipline?

We need to endure the Lord's discipline, remembering that it is God treating us as His own children. When the Lord calls us to repentance, to change your direction, He is treating us as His own child.

Something always amazed me when I was a little boy. There were a lot of kids in the neighborhood meaner than I was, but my mother never one time spanked any of them. What was that all about?! Yes, my mom often gave me some direction with the "board of education." Why? Simple. Because I was hers. She loved me and was responsible for me. My mom wanted me to live in an honorable and right way, so she took what the Bible said about the "rod of correction" quite literally. She did not interpret that Biblical admonition in the least bit symbolically. I did not appreciate her understanding of that Scripture when I was a child, but I certainly do now. My mother loved me, and that is why she disciplined me when I was disobedient and rebellious.

We should treasure repentance because of what it is and what it means. Repentance means that we can turn to God because He has not given up on us. Repentance must also be treasured because of what it does. Repentance brings alignment into our life.

Have you ever driven a very nice car with all the options and features—air conditioning, a great stereo system, comfortable seats—but it has one wheel out of alignment? Boy, isn't that a fun ride? You are either swerving to the right or pulling to the left. You apply the brake, and the car pulls to one side. It is "out of alignment." It is not correctly connecting with the road, and the steering is not balanced.

Likewise, when the Lord calls us to repentance, He is calling us into alignment with Him. This alignment with God is what David refers to as "the everlasting way." Jesus made a similar promise to those who follow Him, "I have come to give you life and to give it to you abundantly." "The way everlasting" is the "abundant life." It truly is the "best life now" and is only found by repenting and aligning ourselves with God. This is the only way to experiencing the "best life now." Not by focusing on ourselves and our desires, but by coming face-to-face with true greatness, which is God. He is perfect love. Aligning our lives on Him is our "best life now." The best life is a life of conformity to Jesus.

> Do not be conformed to this world, but be transformed by the renewal of your mind, that by testing you may discern what is the will of God, what is good and acceptable and perfect.
> (Romans 12:2)

I once heard a preacher say something that I have never forgotten. He said, "God is so good, and God is so kind, and God is so wise that we would choose what He chooses if we had enough sense to choose it." That is not an elegant statement, but it is certainly intelligent.

The best thing we can do is align ourselves with God—the all-knowing, all-wise, all-loving God. He gave his Son for us, and no good thing will He withhold from those who walk with Him. That is truly living. That is "the way everlasting." We should *Treasure* repentance, grateful that God is granting to us a sense of our need because He is calling us to the Kingdom. He is calling us to a path that is the best path.

REPENTANCE MUST BE TIMELY

The second thing we need to understand about repentance is that it must be *timely*. We should not think of our prayer of repentance as something we do from time to time. Repentance needs to be a regular part of our time with the Lord because we regularly need to realign with Him. Day by day, we need to be making sure we are on the path of obedience. We all tend to drift and find ourselves on the wrong road. Regular repentance is how we can stay off those dangerous detours.

Interestingly, the reformers of the 16th & 17th centuries who experienced the great awakening and return to gospel Christianity from ages of formalistic, dead religion were often derided by their enemies as *"repenters."* They were given this title because their lives were characterized by regular repentance.

The closer we walk with Jesus, the closer we stay to Him, the more we see how much and how often we need to repent. Some people become so discouraged, saying, "I'm trying to become a better Christian, but the further along I go, the worse it seems I become." That is a normal experience, not abnormal, because as our God becomes bigger in our eyes, and we see more clearly how glorious He is, the smaller we see ourselves to be. But thankfully, His grace becomes bigger to us as well. The preciousness and powerfulness of His saving grace will become more and more important to our lives as we begin to live more and more in this attitude of repentance.

I recently discovered something so beautiful regarding repentance in reading the 13th Chapter of the Gospel of John. Jesus is celebrating Passover with his disciples and instituting the Lord's supper. But before that takes place, Jesus fills a basin with water, wraps a towel around His waist, and begins to wash the disciples' feet.

> Then he poured water into a basin and began to wash the disciples' feet and to wipe them with the towel that was wrapped around him. He came to Simon Peter, who said to him, "Lord, do you wash my feet?" Jesus answered him, "What I am doing you do not understand now, but afterward you will understand." Peter said to him, "You shall never [ever] wash my feet." Jesus answered him, "If I do not wash you, you have no share with me." Simon Peter said to him, "Lord, not my feet only but also my hands and my head!" (John 13:5-9)

Peter often opened his mouth too quickly, but his heart was full of love for the Lord. Listen to his exclamation, "Lord, if to be partnered with you, I must be washed, then give me a complete bath. Don't stop at my feet!" And what was Jesus' response?

> Jesus said to him, "The one who has bathed [the one who has been completely cleaned] does not need to wash, except for his feet, but is completely clean. And you are clean, but not every one of you." (John 13:10)

Jesus' message to Peter is that His followers must be washed, but washed only once in regeneration. Believers are born again by the washing of the *regeneration*, that is, the renewing of the Holy Spirit (Titus 3:5). In other words, we are only "washed," *born again*, one time. But we have to be cleansed in our walk with Jesus regularly. We have one cleansing in *salvation,* but we must have many, many washings of our feet in *sanctification*. Even though we are walking with Jesus, our feet are still getting dirty. So, in repentance, we must often ask, "Lord, wash my feet again. Cleanse me again. Bring me back into fellowship with You."

Repentance is a crucial part of our GPS, *God's Positioning System*. God works in our hearts to call us into a You-Turn that keeps us in fellowship with Him. Yes, we have a relationship with Him that cannot be broken. We are God's children in our identity, but there are times we get dirty, and we need to be cleansed. That cleansing comes from repentance and, thank God, it is a complete cleansing.

> If we confess our sins, he is faithful
> and just to forgive us our sins and
> to cleanse us from all
> unrighteousness. (1 John 1:9)

REPENTANCE MUST BE THOROUGH

So, our repentance should be *treasured,* and it needs to be *timely,* but it must also be *thorough.* David, in the beautiful song of Psalm 139, pleads with the Lord to investigate his life. "Search my heart, see if there is any wicked way in me."

Perhaps some of you reading these pages may be raising children or may be raising grandchildren. You might ask them, "Have you cleaned your room?"

They quickly answer, "Yeah."

You are not entirely convinced. "You cleaned your room?"

"Oh, yeah. It's done" is the response.

Just then, you notice the door to their room happens to be closed. Now, of course, you love your children, but you don't necessarily completely trust them. Why don't you trust your children? Because you don't trust their parents—namely, you!

We are all sinners, and we know we tend to cover up all sorts of things that we don't want others to see. Your children might say that they have cleaned their room, but you open the door, go inside, and look around. It is amazing how children and teenagers often define what a "clean room" looks like!

As parents or grandparents, we have to do a thorough job of inspecting whether our child has cleaned their room or not. It's the same way with repentance. We have to invite our Heavenly Father into "our room." We need Him to investigate all the recesses of our life—the dark corners, that closet, maybe even peer into that box up on the top shelf. This is the true spirit of repentance. "Lord, search me. Know my heart. Reveal any wicked way in me."

THE FOUR CORNERS OF SIN

1. Sins of Volition

Think of your own heart as having four corners, and those four corners have to do with sin. We need to make sure that we ask the Lord to show us any *sins of volition*. Sins of volition have to do with our thoughts. Many problems begin there, with our thoughts in the hidden chambers of our minds.

> Keep your heart with all vigilance,
> for from it flow the springs of life.
> (Proverbs 4:23)

We must learn to guard and guide our hearts because "the heart" has to do with our thinking process. Sinful thinking is sin, and a repentant spirit in prayer desires the Lord to reveal sins of volition.

2. Sins of Relation

Sins of relation have to do with people. Our relationship with others is part of our relationship with God.

> So if you are offering your gift at the altar and there remember that your brother has something against you, leave your gift there before the altar and go. First be reconciled to your brother, and then come and offer your gift. (Matthew 5:23-24)

Jesus teaches that our relationship with our brother or sister is more important than going through the observances of religion. Therefore, we must search our hearts. How are we relating to others? Is there anyone who has something against me? Is there a need to forgive somebody who has wronged me?

In Matthew 6, Jesus taught us to pray, "Forgive us our trespasses as we forgive those who trespass against us."

Repentance is also expressed in the act of forgiveness. Our attitude should be, "Lord, don't let me hold on to these wrongs. You haven't held onto *my* wrongs. Do I think I'm better than you? You have released me; I must release them. Lord, you sacrificed yourself to free me of my debt. Help me to free others."

3. Sins of Commission

We must also ask the Lord to reveal to our hearts any *sins of commission*. Sins of commission are actions. Things that have been done.

> Everyone who makes a practice of sinning also practices lawlessness; sin is lawlessness. (1 John 3:4)

We transgress the law by things that we do, by actions we have taken. Sins are defined as the breaking of God's law. We must ask Him to help us search our hearts regarding possible transgressions. "Lord, if I have sinned, if I have done something wrong in violating your Law, show that to me."

Sins of commission also include, not just things we have *done,* but also things we have *said.* We violate the Law of God when we wrong another person by *saying* what we should not have said or by *not saying* what we should have said.

> Let no corrupting talk come out of
> your mouths, but only such as is
> good for building up, as fits the
> occasion, that it may give grace to
> those who hear. (Ephesians 4:29)

Sometimes the Lord, as the Good Physician, in carrying out His spiritual examination, shines His light into our mouths! The existence of any heart problem is often revealed there because it is out of the mouth that our heart speaks. (Matt. 12:34).

4. Sins of Omission

Sin is not just something we have done that we shouldn't have done. Equally as wrong are *sins of omission*. This is when we don't do something that we should have done. As the Lord grants us the gift of repentance, His goal is not only to take away things from our lives that are bad but, just as importantly, to add to our lives the qualities that are best.

> So whoever knows the right thing to do and fails to do it, for him it is sin. (James 4:17)

God's *investigation* of our heart leads to God's *invitation* to our heart. Listen to His amazing invitation:

> "Come now, let us reason together, says the Lord: though your sins are like scarlet, they shall be as white as snow; though they are red like crimson, they shall become like wool." (Isaiah 1:18)

God's call to repentance is when He says, "This is my invitation. *Come to Me.*" God only gives us an *investigation* to then offer us the greatest of all *invitations*—an invitation to Himself. Repentance is an incredible opportunity to experience the King and to walk in the ways of the Kingdom. This is our Lord's invitation to the "best life" that we can possibly have.

Bertha Smith was a tremendous missionary and an incredible servant of the Lord. Her life was in danger many times as she served the Lord overseas for several decades. When Miss

Smith left the mission field and returned to the United States, she soon became involved in an amazing and unique ministry of prayer. In her "retirement," people would come from everywhere to her residence in a remote part of South Carolina so that she would pray with them. Missionaries, pastors, evangelists—people from all walks of life would come to see her.

Typically, after they arrived, they would have a personal discussion and read through some applicable passages of the Bible. Eventually, Bertha would give the individuals a piece of red paper and tell them that she was going to leave them alone for a time of reflection. She would ask them to pray that the Lord search them and show them what was in their heart. Then, as they repented, she instructed them to write their sins on those red sheets of paper. Sometimes it wouldn't be just one sheet of paper; it would be *sheets* of paper.

Then Bertha would say to them, "After you've prayed over that piece of paper and confessed every sin to the Lord, I want you to come over here, crumble them up, and put them in this trash can." All the red pieces of paper were set on fire and burned to ashes. She then led them in a prayer of rejoicing in the Lord and praising Him for His forgiveness and restoration.

You cannot imagine the breakthroughs that happened in that woman's home because people took the time to simply reflect, write it down, repent, and agree with God.

But here is the good news. We do not need a trash can for this experience to happen. We do not need red pieces of paper. We do not even need a pen. Repenting in that way is helpful, yes, but it is not necessary because we have a place where we can take our sin. We can take our sin to the Lord Jesus Christ—to His crimson blood. He washes it clean, and He buries it in the sea of forgetfulness. He remembers our sins no more. Now that is a fantastic gift!

That gift is available right now. Go to the Lord in prayer, asking Him to shine His glorious light into your heart and reveal to you any sin, known or unknown. Through His grace, you can experience the gift of His repentance, giving your sin to Jesus, who will take it away forever.

REPENT

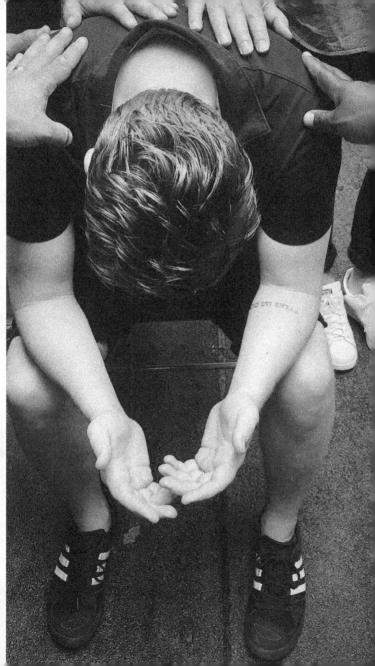

P

R

INTERCESSION

S

M

3

IsN'T IT AMAZING THAT NO MATTER WHERE
we are, in just a moment of time, we can cross
into the very presence of the Lord through
prayer? He hears us all, and He hears us each
one. What a mighty God we serve!

Over time, our prayer lives can become
mundane and predictable—praying at about the
same time of day and practically the same
manner. The Bible teaches us that we should
pray using all types of prayer, and the Lord is
pleased when, through these varieties of
expression, we come before Him. By using the
word P. R. I. S. M., we have a guide that can
help us incorporate the various aspects of
prayer—*Praise, Repentance, Intercession,
Specific Requests*, and *Meditation*. In this
chapter, we want to focus on the incredible gift
the Lord has given us in the ministry of
intercession.

Several years ago, a young woman began attending our church, and after a period of time, she came to know the Lord as her Savior. God started to change her life in mighty ways. Eventually, she met a godly man, they fell in love and were married. A few years into their marriage, this dear lady was sitting in her car at an intersection of a busy highway near our city airport. Two vehicles were traveling from the same direction on the four-lane road that would cross in front of her. One of the cars suddenly changed lanes too quickly, clipping the back end of the one in front. This caused that automobile to go airborne and land directly on top of the car in which the woman was sitting. Tragically, she was killed instantly.

Word got out quickly about the accident and her husband, becoming aware, immediately tried to get in touch with her. When his wife did not answer her phone, the husband rushed to the scene of the accident. Arriving there, he was informed by officers that his sweet wife had been killed in the terrible crash. Of course, he was absolutely devastated and dazed by the trauma of what had happened.

As he gazed at the scene in front of him, trying to comprehend what he was seeing, he noticed a person sitting on the side of the road, weeping. When he asked who it was, he was told, "That is the man who was driving the car that clipped the other vehicle and caused the accident."

What happened next was truly an amazing display of God's love and grace in a believer's heart. The man who had just lost his beloved wife walked over to the man who had caused her death, sat down beside him, and embraced him saying, "I forgive you. Please let me pray for you." He prayed over the man and asked for God to give him strength to endure what had just taken place. Miraculous.

Only the love of Jesus Christ can give the kind of grace that causes us to think of others in the midst of our deepest heartache, even to those who may have caused the pain. That is the power of God's love. The grace for a grieving husband to hold in his arms the person responsible for his wife's death, praying for God to heal and help, is an unworldly grace that can only come from the Lord. It is the grace of *intercession*.

If you are familiar with the Book of Ezekiel, you are aware that it contains some passages that are somewhat difficult to understand. However, Ezekiel also shares messages that are crystal clear in clarity and just as clearly amazing. This is especially true concerning the topic of intercession. In Ezekiel 22:29, the Lord speaks to his prophet, saying:

> The people of the land have
> practiced extortion and committed
> robbery. They have oppressed the
> poor and needy, and have extorted
> from the sojourner without justice.
> (Ezekiel 22:29)

Israel's culture was quite religious when it came to sacred observances, but it was a society far from the knowledge of God and His heart. The people of Israel did not know God. But they did know extortion, robbery, oppression of the poor and needy, and abuse of the sojourner. They were an unjust people. Listen to the Lord as He describes perhaps the greatest tragedy of all regarding the condition of the nation:

> And I sought for a man among
> them who should build up the wall
> and stand in the breach before me
> for the land, that I should not
> destroy it, but I found none.
> Therefore I have poured out my
> indignation upon them. I have
> consumed them with the fire of my
> wrath. I have returned their way
> upon their heads, declares the Lord
> God." (Ezekiel 22:30-31)

God had seen terrible, wicked injustice, and ungodliness among His people Israel. Because of this, God, in His justice, had brought judgment down upon them. But notice the terrible tragedy of unconcern that the Lord reveals, *"I was looking for a man who would build up the wall, who would stand in the breach before me, that I should not destroy it, but I found none."* What a terrible reality! Not one person would stir up himself to intercede on behalf of the people for their wickedness. No one cared enough to intercede. Not one.

THE PRINCIPLE OF INTERCESSION

From these verses in Ezekiel, we learn some astounding things about the principle of intercession. The literal meaning of the English word "intercession" comes from two Latin words meaning "to go between." Prayers of intercession are prayers that are meant "to go between." Intercessory prayer, then, is coming to God on another person's behalf. I like to think of intercession as *kneeling down to stand up* for others. Of course, this doesn't mean we have to literally be on our knees or stand on our feet before we can pray a prayer of intercession. However, it does mean, in a real sense, that through prayer, we are "standing in" for someone else.

In the year 2000, I experienced a season of an extended illness. During those seven months, I could not speak clearly because of a weakness in the muscles controlling my voice and articulation. I could not teach or carry on conversations for more than a few minutes. It was an extremely difficult time, to say the least.

I was so grateful for the numerous prayer gatherings called on my behalf. On one occasion, some local pastors committed to come to our church and conduct a prayer service for me in the sanctuary. After the service, one of the pastors excitedly called me on the phone and exclaimed, "Sam, if I have ever heard anyone prayed for in my life, it was you in that service today!" My pastor-friend went on to tell me how one particular pastor had to have been led to pray for me. Standing to his feet, he called out in a loud voice, "Lord, I am *praying* for Sam Polson. Lord, I am *standing* for Sam Polson. Lord, *I am* Sam Polson, and I'm asking you to heal me."

My friend's testimony about the prayer of that pastor brought me to tears. How I thank God for the way he, and so many countless other believers, interceded to the Lord on my behalf! It was a scary, dark time, and I am eternally grateful for those who "stood in the gap" for me in faith-filled intercession.

We should never lose sight of what a privilege it is to be the person who prays to Almighty God on behalf of others. Intercession is a privilege for so many reasons, not the least of which is the incredible reality that intercessory prayer is based on Jesus' ministry.

> For there is one God, and there is
> one mediator between God and
> men, the man Christ Jesus.
> (1 Timothy 2:5)

There is one Mediator, and only one who came from God on our behalf. And there is only one who can bring us to the Father who sent Him, and that is His Son, Jesus Christ. The Apostle Peter reminds believers through the ages of that incredible truth, "For Christ also suffered, once for sin, the righteous for the unrighteous, that he might bring us to God..." (1 Pet. 3:18).

But Jesus' ministry of mediation is not just limited to what He did in the past. It also involves what Jesus is doing in the *present*. Intercession is literally at-the-heart of our Lord's ministry today. Some people have the idea that Jesus went back to heaven and is now just sitting on the throne next to the Father, tapping his foot until the Father says to him, "Okay, Son. You can return now and bring your brothers and sisters home." Nothing could be further from the truth.

Jesus has been actively working in a ministry since the moment He returned to heaven. The writer of the Epistle to the Hebrews tells us that Jesus' ministry has been that of an intercessor for nearly 2000 years.

> Since then we have a great high
> priest who has passed through the
> heavens, Jesus, the Son of God, let
> us hold fast our confession. For we
> do not have a high priest who is
> unable to sympathize with our
> weaknesses, but one who in every
> respect has been tempted as we are,
> yet without sin. Let us then with
> confidence draw near to the throne
> of grace, that we may receive mercy
> and find grace to help in time of
> need. (Hebrews 4:14-16)

Jesus' present work is the ministry of an intercessor. He is praying on behalf of His people. He is our High Priest before the presence of God. In the Old Testament, the high priest wore a breastplate decorated with 12 precious stones, each stone representing one of Israel's 12 tribes. As the high priest came into the temple of God, he wore, upon his heart, the 12 symbols of God's people.

All of that imagery previewed the work of the ultimate High Priest to come. Jesus has offered Himself as the perfect sacrifice through His death on the cross, risen from the dead, ascended back to heaven, and now has entered the temple in heaven representing the people He came to save. Our great High Priest doesn't need a breastplate on His chest because our names are in His heart. The only things Jesus took back to heaven with him from Earth were the scars in His body. Everything else He left behind, including the seamless coat. Jesus' scars are the eternal symbols of His love and sacrifice. Now He is in heaven interceding for us.

When we pray on behalf of others, we are entering into the very ministry of Jesus. He allows us to share with Him in His work. On Earth, when we serve in His Name, we are doing His work. He is with us as we go. When we pray in the Spirit, we join with Jesus in His work in heaven. What a Savior we have!

It is difficult to grasp everything that this ministry of intercession includes. That is okay. We hold as absolutely true many things that we do not fully understand, but we know that these beautiful and wonderful certainties are ours to claim and experience by faith. Kneeling on behalf of others here on Earth, we enter into Jesus' spiritual work that He is carrying out in heaven. Praying on behalf of others is such an incredible ministry! We must never diminish it. What more priceless gift could we ever give to one another than the gift of our prayers?

Yes, we have an incredible ministry through intercessory prayer for others, but how do we actually do it? Let us consider three practices and purposes of intercessory prayer.

1. Praying for the welfare
of others

In Genesis 18:23-33, Abraham interceded to God on behalf of his nephew Lot and his family. It is a fantastic story. The Lord came down from heaven and actually had a meal with Abraham. After the meal, the Lord revealed to Abraham that he had come to personally evaluate the moral and spiritual condition of Sodom and all the cities of the plain. Immediately, Abraham began to intercede:

> Then Abraham drew near and said, "Will you indeed sweep away the righteous with the wicked? Suppose there are fifty righteous within the city. Will you then sweep away the place and not spare it for the fifty righteous who are in it? Far be it from you to do such a thing, to put the righteous to death with the wicked, so that the righteous fare as the wicked! Far be that from you! Shall not the Judge of all the earth do what is just?" And the Lord said, "If I find at Sodom fifty righteous in the city, I will spare the whole place for their sake."
>
> Abraham answered and said, "Behold, I have undertaken to speak

to the Lord, I who am but dust and ashes. Suppose five of the fifty righteous are lacking. Will you destroy the whole city for lack of five?" And he said, "I will not destroy it if I find forty-five there." Again he spoke to him and said, "Suppose forty are found there." He answered, "For the sake of forty I will not do it." Then he said, "Oh let not the Lord be angry, and I will speak. Suppose thirty are found there." He answered, "I will not do it, if I find thirty there." He said, "Behold, I have undertaken to speak to the Lord. Suppose twenty are found there." He answered, "For the sake of twenty I will not destroy it." Then he said, "Oh let not the Lord be angry, and I will speak again but this once. Suppose ten are found there." He answered, "For the sake of ten I will not destroy it." And the Lord went his way, when he had finished speaking to Abraham, and Abraham returned to his place.

(Genesis 18:23-33)

Sadly, in the entire population of Sodom and Gomorrah's cities, not even ten righteous people could be found, and the judgment of God came. However, God had heard Abraham's prayers of intercession, and He sent two angels to rescue Lot and his family. The angel said to Lot, "You must leave this place because I can do nothing until you are gone." Lot did not understand that it was the intervention of his uncle Abraham's intercession that saved his life and the lives of his wife and daughters. We are told that Abraham walked from his tent and, looking toward the plain, saw the smoke rising from the cities. At that moment, Abraham did not know that God had held back His judgment until Lot and his family were safely delivered out of that city. Lot's safety was a direct result of Abraham's prayers of intercession.

Likewise, our prayers of intercession for others often accomplish much more than we may ever recognize in this life. The intercession of God's children to their Father in heaven is incredibly influential on Earth. It is a good and powerful thing to pray for the welfare of others. It is also essential to intercede for the welfare of our country. The Bible says in 2 Chronicles 7:14,

> If my people who are called by my
> name humble themselves, and pray
> and seek my face and turn from
> their wicked ways, then I will hear
> from heaven and will forgive their
> sin and heal their land.

The Lord calls on us as His people to intercede for the nation in which we live. We are told by our Heavenly Father to pray for our country, our city, and our community. God's command to His people living in Babylon, the city of their captivity, is timeless in its application to all generations of believers wherever they live:

> But seek the welfare of the city where I have sent you into exile, and pray to the Lord on its behalf, for in its welfare you will find your welfare. (Jeremiah 29:7)

Amazing. God instructed His people to pray for the very nation that had taken them captive. They were told to pray that the peace of that country might be their peace. As citizens of heaven temporarily living on Earth, what are we challenged to pray for? Listen to Paul's instructions for us:

> First of all, then, I urge that supplications, prayers, inter-cessions, and thanksgivings be made for all people, for kings and all who are in high positions, that we may lead a peaceful and quiet life, godly and dignified in every way. This is good, and it is pleasing in the sight of God our Savior, who desires all people to be saved and

to come to the knowledge of the truth. (1 Timothy 2:1-4)

When Paul wrote these words to the churches in Asia Minor, the government was *Rome*, and the emperor was *Nero*. Think about the implications of that. Intercession is not just to be offered for godly leaders and righteous governments. Instead, we are commanded to pray for a pagan culture for the purpose of our sacred mission. Notice, Paul said to pray "that we may lead a peaceful and quiet life, godly and dignified in every way." The principle shared here is that we are to pray for our government and its leaders so that through the peace of the land, we might, by our living witness, see people saved and come to the knowledge of the truth of the gospel.

We have a very important mission, and that mission is the salvation of eternal souls. For the advancement of that mission, we are called to pray for those who have authority on Earth. Their authority is only a *delegated* authority. God's authority is above all authorities. We take our pleas to *The Ultimate* "Supreme Court," praying that even in this society we might be able to live out our faith and be a light to our nation and the nations of the Earth. (Even if that society may seem to us like Babylon at times, and treat us as captives.)

God desires that people experience the eternal freedom found only in the knowledge of Jesus as King of Kings and Lord of Lords. The expansion of that Kingdom of our Lord involves the most intense battle imaginable. Our prayers of intercession should also include those involved in the warfare that is the greatest of all warfare—*spiritual* warfare.

2. Praying for those in spiritual warfare

There is an amazing story recorded in the 17th Chapter of Exodus that perfectly illustrates the ministry of intercessory prayer on behalf of those involved in spiritual warfare for the Lord's cause. As the people of Israel were fighting the Amalekites, Moses went up to the top of the mountain that overlooked the battlefield. When Moses' arms were stretched toward heaven, the Israelites would begin winning the battle. However, when his arms came down in fatigue, the battle turned against God's people. It didn't take long for someone to figure out what was going on. They must have cried, "Keep Moses' hands up!" The Bible says that Aaron and Hur came to stand beside Moses as the battle raged below, keeping his arms raised heavenward. Through this story, God shows us that *He alone* gives the victory and that victory is given *through* the ministry of intercession.

Likewise, when God's people are in spiritual warfare, as they labor in the cause of Christ, we are called to pray for them with intercessory prayers. In the midst of spiritual warfare, we should always pray for the witness of others. We must put on the armor of God, but if we wear it in a spirit of self-confidence, that armor is not going to provide adequate protection. We cannot forget how essential the attitude of prayer truly is in response to spiritual warfare. It is the power of our dependence on the Lord that actually empowers that prayer.

Ephesians 6:10-17 speaks to us about the armor of God that we are to put on daily in preparation for our battle with the Enemy. We must do this deliberately, but we absolutely must also do this *prayerfully*,

> ...and take the helmet of salvation, and the sword of the Spirit, which is the word of God, praying at all times in the Spirit, with all prayer and supplication. To that end, keep alert with all perseverance, making supplication for all the saints, and also for me, that words may be given to me in opening my mouth boldly to proclaim the mystery of the gospel, for which I am an

ambassador in chains, that I may declare it boldly, as I ought to speak. (Ephesians 6:17-20)

How did Jesus come against the devil? He quoted scripture, declaring, "It is written." We need to learn to *fight like Jesus* by using God's Word. But it doesn't stop there. "Take the sword of the Spirit, which is the word of God, *praying at all times* in the Spirit, with all prayer and supplication." And "To that end, keep alert with all perseverance, making supplication for all the saints..."

You see, it is not just us who are involved in warfare; it's raging for *all* the family of God, for *all* the soldiers of the Lord. Paul says especially, "As you are praying, *pray also for me*, that words may be given to me in opening my mouth boldly to proclaim the mystery of the gospel, for which I am an ambassador in chains, that I may declare it boldly, as I ought to speak."

Paul is in chains, and he knows that he will soon be going before Nero. He is fully aware that he will be walking right into the heart of darkness, the mouth of the Lion. Paul's greatest desire is this, "I want to be bold, to share the truth. And I need you to pray for me."

We need to pray for our witness and the witness of others because apart from the Lord, we can do nothing. Not one thing. Do you know what *"nothing"* is? Nothing is a zero with the border erased. Without God, we can't even do zero. But *with* him, we can do all things. We can be as *meek as lambs,* but we can also be the righteous, who are as *bold as lions*.

We need to pray, especially during these challenging times of increasing darkness, that we will be gospel speaking people. We need to keep sharing, again and again, our theme of the gospel of Jesus Christ. We must keep proclaiming this gospel truth with persistence. Essential to the persistent witness of the gospel is the persistent work of intercession. Intercession is work. Remember what Samuel the prophet said,

> For the Lord will not forsake his people, for his great name's sake, because it has pleased the Lord to make you a people for himself. Moreover, as for me, far be it from me that I should sin against the Lord by ceasing to pray for you, and I will instruct you in the good and the right way. (1 Samuel 12:22-23)

Samuel was the judge of the people of God, and he knew there would be a new leader for the people, a king. But he says, "I will not give up my first calling, which is to be a man of prayer for you, and to continue teaching you the ways of the Lord." That is an incredible passage. My friends, we must keep praying. We must never give up this ministry of intercession.

George Mueller was a man significantly used by God in England during the mid-1800s for the establishment of many orphanages. At one time, 5,000 children were under his care. George determined that he would trust in God alone to provide. He did not ask of others; he asked only of God.

Mueller kept a journal of his prayer requests and his intercessions. He documented every prayer, and then how those prayers were answered. When he died, friends retrieved his prayer journals and discovered 10,000 entries where George had made note of the answering of those prayers.

But there was one prayer request that had a blank beside it. That prayer request was for George Mueller's brother, for whom he had prayed for over 50 years to come to know Jesus.

At George Mueller's funeral, his brother trusted Jesus Christ as his Lord and Savior. No doubt there were "hallelujahs" offered up by George Mueller in heaven! The Lord had heard his persistent prayers of intercession over the years and answered them.

Our prayers are timeless. We may not see the answer in our lifetime, but our prayers live on after our time on Earth. We must never forget to maintain persistence in our prayer life because our prayers last forever.

3. Praying with sensitivity to listen

Finally, we must make sure that while we are praying, we pray to be very sensitive to what we are sensing in our spirit. Why do I say that? Recall what the Lord said seven times to the churches in the Book of Revelation: "He who has an ear, let him hear what the Spirit says to the churches." The Lord says that seven times in two chapters.

Certainly, we can hear what the Spirit is saying through the Book that He inspired. However, the Lord also speaks Spirit to spirit. He can make His Word come alive to us and give us perceptions that we might not even be able to understand, but we can sense, deeply. We might not fully understand what our spirit is sensing from the Lord, but we must respond in intercession and talk to Him about it. Countless believers can bear witness to this reality.

One night, many years ago, my wife, Susan, awoke at 3 am. She couldn't understand what was troubling her, but something was wrong. She knew someone was in need of prayer, and that burden was on her heart. She couldn't name who the person was, but she rose and went into our family room and got on her knees and began to pray. A few minutes later, the phone rang, and it was the wife of a member of our staff, calling to say her husband had just been taken to the hospital and was in serious condition. God did not reveal to Susan who she was praying for, but she knew she had to pray for someone. The Spirit was leading her, Spirit to spirit.

In the year 2000, I was hospitalized for surgery for the same illness I mentioned earlier in the chapter. A friend called me just before the surgery. He said, "Sam, it's going to be okay. You don't have to worry. It's answered." This call took place on Sunday at about 1 pm as I was being prepped for the surgery the following day.

My friend said, "I just came from visiting a church, where I attended a Sunday school class." He continued, "This is the first time I have ever attended that church. I just felt that I was supposed to visit there today." He went on, "I was in class, and at the end of the class they were taking prayer requests, so I raised my hand and said, 'I know you don't know him, but I wish that you would pray for a friend of mine, Pastor Sam.'"

My friend then told me this, "Sam, this elderly couple in the corner started sobbing, and then they walked over and told me this:

'Yesterday we were sitting on the porch having our devotions, looking out on a beautiful day, and it just came onto our hearts to pray for someone.' The elderly man said through tears, 'While we were praying, a name came to me, and I wrote it down on this piece of paper.' The man then pulled out the piece of paper and showed it to my friend. On it was written the words, 'Pastor Sam.'"

Think of the implications of God's guidance in that entire experience. These people did not know me, but they were prompted by the Spirit to pray for me. Then, the same the Spirit sent my friend into that Sunday school class so he could request prayer, where he would meet two people who had been called by the Holy Spirit to pray an intercessory prayer on my behalf. If this were not enough, my friend was prompted by the Spirit to contact me and share those incredibly encouraging words, "Brother, it's going to be okay." I have to say, I felt a whole lot better about my upcoming surgery after that call!

God can do amazing things through intercession. And as we speak to the Lord in prayer for others, we must also be careful to *listen...Spirit to spirit.*

INTERCEDE

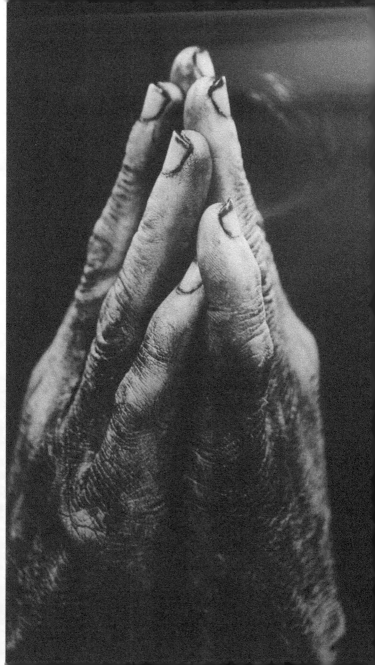

P
R
I

SPECIFIC REQUESTS

M

4

THERE IS NO BETTER USE FOR THE HUMAN voice than to praise our Creator and Redeemer. When we pray, we worship God, and more than any other area of our lives, we want to avoid getting into a rut with our seasons of worship. An effective way to make sure that our seasons of prayer stay fresh with various applications is to use our word *PRISM* as a guide.

In the previous chapters, we have defined this helpful acrostic for prayer by noting that the "P" stands for *praise* during prayer times. "R" reminds us of the need to *repent* regularly. The "I" emphasizes the prayer focus of *intercession*, which reminds us to *stand up* for others when we *kneel* before the Lord, taking the needs of others to our Heavenly Father.

In this chapter, we will focus on the letter "S" in *PRISM*, which stands for *specific requests*, or as the King James Version renders this concept of prayer, "supplications."

It is easy to fall into a prayer pattern in which we use many words and phrases in communication with the Lord but not specifically ask Him for anything. Prayers that rarely ask God to work in specific ways are not the expression of prayer that we are challenged in the Bible to offer to Him.

When I was in seminary many years ago, there was a story that was legendary on campus about a retired missionary to Asia. Grace had served on that continent for over 50 years. When she was physically no longer able to stay in Asia (and because of the ever-increasing persecution), she returned to the states to teach courses at the university. Grace lived in a little apartment, located directly below one of the graduate halls where the men were studying.

One night, several of those students got together for a prayer service in a room that was right above her apartment. These young seminarians prayed very loud, long, and theologically precise prayers to God about His awesome holiness, His glory, and His splendor. Finally, this elderly missionary, a devoted believer in prayer, could stand it no longer. In the middle of their prayer meeting, she found a broom and began banging on the ceiling of her apartment while crying out in a loud voice, "Ask Him to do something! Ask Him to do something!" She was tired of hearing them pray all the big and theologically accurate words but not actually asking God to do something—anything! That is good advice for our prayer time as well. We need to make sure we include *specific requests* in our times of prayer. We need to ask God to do *specific things*.

In Matthew's following passage, we are taught the importance of bringing our specific requests to God by the greatest of all encouragers regarding prayer— the Lord Jesus Christ.

Most of us are aware that Matthew, Chapter 7, is part of what is commonly known as the *Sermon on the Mount*. Throughout this message, Jesus provides words of instruction and encouragement to His disciples regarding many subjects. However, none are more powerful than His challenge regarding the importance of boldness and confidence in our prayers to God.

> "Ask, and it will be given to you; seek, and you will find; knock, and it will be opened to you. For everyone who asks receives, and the one who seeks finds, and to the one who knocks it will be opened. Or which one of you, if his son asks him for bread, will give him a stone? Or if he asks for a fish, will

> give him a serpent? If you then, who
> are evil, know how to give good gifts
> to your children, how much more
> will your Father who is in heaven
> give good things to those who ask
> him!" (Matthew 7:7-11)

One of Jesus' greatest purposes during His ministry was to introduce His disciples to His Father. Of course, they had been taught throughout their lives about the greatness and power of the God of their fathers. But Jesus wanted His disciples to know His Father as their Father as well. Yes, he is infinite, but He is also intimate. God loves them personally and completely, and anything that concerns them is of concern to Him. The Heavenly Father's heart is *for them*, and therefore, *for their good*. Jesus expressed this by a comparison that was as irresistible in its logic as it was intimate in its intention.

> "If you then, who are evil, know how
> to give good gifts to your children,
> how much more will your Father
> who is in heaven give good things to
> those who ask him!" (Matthew 7:11)

Notice again what Jesus said, "...your Father who is in heaven..." Does that remind you of something Jesus said in an earlier part of this

Sermon on the Mount as He shared with His disciples a model of prayer?

> Pray then like this:
> "Our Father in heaven,
> hallowed be your name.
> (Matthew 6:9)

We are so familiar with the statement, "Our Father in heaven," that we fail to remember how startling a statement that truly was. When Jesus told his disciples to pray "Our Father in heaven," it was revolutionary because never had anyone instructed people to refer to God as their personal father until this moment. Never.

In the Old Testament, God is sometimes referred to as the Father of the Nation Israel. But never does anyone in all of Scripture nor any other recorded statements made by God's people, refer to God as our "Father." What Jesus is sharing about the relationship His disciples have to the Father is startling and without precedence.

However, the *only* way Jesus ever referred to God was always "Father," except for one time, when from the cross, He cried out, "My God, why have you forsaken me?" In that awful moment, the Son spoke as the sacrifice for sin and the substitute for sinners, suffering the wrath of an offended God that *we* justly deserved.

Jesus always refers to God as "My Father" or "Our Father," and here He gives an invitation. He tells us that we can bring our request to Almighty God and know that we are speaking to our Heavenly Father. Now, allow that to sink in for a moment. The One who is creator and sustainer of all things—almighty, eternal, omniscient, omnipresent, omnipotent God—we can call, "Father." Jesus uses the word "Abba." Abba is a very tender word for father, having to do with family. The closest translation we have in our English language today would be, "Dad."

Since that is the relationship we have with God, Jesus wants us to know that we can come to Him in prayer with a security and confidence that we are not outsiders intruding on the time of a harsh and uncaring despot. No. We come before God, beloved by Him, as His dear sons and daughters. Anything that is on our hearts is important to Him. We can open our hearts and share with Him freely about all our concerns and all our needs. He loves us and cares for us. He is our dear Father. How could we possibly imagine that such a Father would begrudge our asking Him for the things we need?

Those of you reading these words, who happen to be parents or grandparents, when Christmas is around-the-corner, do you reluctantly say to yourself, "Oh no, Christmas is coming. I guess I have to do my duty and buy something for these kids and grandkids of mine. They will be expecting something from me *again* this year?" Absolutely not. No one who is a loving parent ever thinks like that.

When our kids were growing up, my wife Susan would have to warn me that she was going to hide our credit cards because I would tend to go crazy buying things for our children! A parent doesn't give gifts to his or her children out of a sense of "duty." A parent gives lovingly out of "devotion."

Now, if we as sinful people feel *that* devoted to our children, Jesus asks,

> Or which one of you, if his son asks him for bread, will give him a stone? Or if he asks for a fish, will give him a serpent?
> (Matthew 7:9-10)

Of course, we would never give a stone or a serpent. And since we, as sinners, would never think of doing that to our children, how much more can we trust God with our specific requests? How much more can we truly believe that we can ask Him for anything? If it concerns us, it concerns our Heavenly Father.

BASIC NEEDS

I love the way Jesus teaches us how we can ask our Father God for the most basic things in life,

> "Pray then like this: 'Our father who is in heaven... Give us this day our daily bread...'" (Matthew 6:11)

I once watched a program about the excavations of the ancient city of Pompeii. In 79 AD, the volcano Mount Vesuvius, located on the west coast of Italy, erupted, spewing volcanic ash and poisonous gasses down upon the city of Pompeii and Herculaneum. As they excavated those cities, buried beneath the volcanic ash, many buildings had remained much as they had been on the day of the eruption. They determined that one particular building was a bakery. Actual loaves of bread were perfectly preserved and had remained almost unchanged for over 1900 years. They turned the loaves over and found initials marked on the bottom. This meant that people had daily accounts at the bakery. Every morning they would come to get their *daily bread* that the baker had carefully prepared.

So, when Jesus encourages us to pray to the Father for our daily bread, He is referring to a practice known all over the ancient world—a timeless reminder of how simple and specific our requests to the Lord should be for all our daily needs. We should pray with such confidence that it is as if our Heavenly Father has already placed our initials on what we request. Can we possibly doubt that the Lord has our initials on the provision of our daily needs when our initials are inscribed in the scars of love on His Son's hands and feet? How can we think for one moment that God is not concerned about us? We shouldn't.

> He who did not spare his own Son
> but gave him up for us all, how will
> he not also with him graciously give
> us all things? (Romans 8:32)

If God, our Father, were going to hold back anything from us, it would have been His beloved Son, Jesus. But if God did not hold back Jesus to meet our *deepest need*, He certainly will not be unwilling to meet our *daily needs*. Having supplied our souls with the Bread of Life, He will never withhold our daily bread from our bodies.

ASKING, SEEKING, KNOCKING

If we believe that we can pray for our daily bread, how should we be praying every day? Well, Jesus tells us to pray like this—*asking, seeking, and knocking.* He is describing the practice of *active rest*. This means we should develop a lifestyle of asking and resting. We ask because we rest in God's goodwill to us. We rest in God's care and concern. We do not have to wonder whether God has good intentions for us or not. We can rest in the fact of who He is, our Heavenly Father. Out of that confident rest in God's care, comes our confidence in continual prayer.

Many times, we do not rest because we do not ask. Sometimes we worry because we have not passed our burdens onto the Lord. We have not released them to Him. Someone has jokingly asked, "Why should we pray when we can worry?" Funny, but no. The cure for worry is prayer— talking to God, asking, and resting.

> "Therefore I tell you, do not be anxious about your life, what you will eat or what you will drink, nor about your body, what you will put on. Is not life more than food, and the body more than clothing? Look at the birds of the air: they neither sow nor reap nor gather into barns, and yet your heavenly Father feeds them. Are you not of more value than they?"
> (Matthew 6:25-26)

And the answer to Jesus' question is, "Yes!" Are we not, as human beings, more important than animals? Yes! Are we not the redeemed children of God, more important to the Father than the birds? Of course! If God takes care of the birds, will He not take care of us? Do you see how Jesus is reasoning with us to help us understand just how much our Heavenly Father loves and cares for us?

> And which of you by being anxious can add a single hour to his span of life? And why are you anxious about clothing? Consider the lilies of the field, how they grow: they neither toil nor spin, yet I tell you, even Solomon in all his glory was not arrayed like one of these. But if God so clothes the grass of the field, which today is alive and tomorrow is thrown into the oven, will he not much more clothe you, O you of little faith?
> (Matthew 6:27-30)

Jesus is detailing the things that we tend to worry about and showing us, in a very kind way, how ridiculous it is to worry about these things once we understand how good our Heavenly Father is. He loves us. He cares for us. Our prayers can rest on this.

The God who cares for us also cares for others. Listen to Jesus as He continues His message about confidence in the Father's loving care:

> "So whatever you wish that others
> would do to you, do also to them, for
> this is the Law and the Prophets."
> (Matthew 7:12)

We call this verse of Scripture the *Golden Rule*, but it seems out of place at first glance. What is Jesus communicating here? He is teaching us that if our Father in heaven is concerned about the things that concern us, we should also be concerned about the things that concern others.

What if the *Golden Rule* measured our prayers? How would our prayers measure up? How often do we sincerely pray for the needs of others?

THE CAUSES OF GOD

So, what about God's concerns? I am not talking about God's *worries* because God never worries. Whatever the situation, He's got it. My question is, do we pray about the things that are on *God's heart*? God has plans and purposes and priorities that He has revealed to us in His Word. Our specific requests in prayer then should reflect the causes of God on Earth. This means that the interests of God should remain ever-present in our lives, and that we should bring the causes of the Father before Him in our times of prayer.

Also, *specific requests* are not to be sporadic requests but persistent requests.

> For everyone who asks receives, and the one who seeks finds, and to the one who knocks it will be opened.
> (Matthew 7:8)

Notice that the verbs "ask," "seek," and "knock" are all in *present tense*. This means to *keep on asking. Keep on seeking. Keep on knocking.* God strengthens our prayer through our persistent praying. Prayer changes things, and more than changing things, prayer changes us. We need to keep on praying, without ceasing, because this persistence in prayer helps us grow in godliness, becoming more like the Lord as we pray about the things on our hearts and His heart. Prayer is not just about getting things changed, but getting *ourselves* changed too. Transformation happens in our lives in ways we are not even aware of due to our consistent prayer.

Paul tells us in Romans 8:29 that God's great purpose in our lives is to conform us to the image of His Son. What is Jesus like? We have no record at all of His physical appearance, but we do know, very clearly, the characteristics that defined him—the fruit of the Spirit.

> But the fruit of the Spirit is love, joy, peace, patience, kindness, goodness, faithfulness, gentleness, self-control; against such things there is no law. (Galatians 5:22-23)

This is what Jesus is like, and it is this image that the Father wants imprinted on all His children.

So, how does this happen? Do we have to take a class in every one of these qualities of the fruit of the Spirit in order to produce them? Of course not. These qualities are the *overflow* of the character of Jesus. Jesus is contagious, and spending time with Him causes us to be *infected* with these qualities. They are passed onto us by the impact of being in His presence in prayerful worship.

If we are concerned about being more loving or more joyful, if we want to be more long-suffering, kinder, more faithful, more gentle, and have more self-control, *then pray*. These are the qualities that God is concerned about, so these are things that should consume our prayer life. As we bring these desires before God in prayer—to emanate the fruit of the

Spirit—to be like Jesus, He produces them in our lives.

THE CAUSES OF GOD
IN OUR WORLD

What is God concerned about in our world? How often do we pray about *His causes*? He is a just God, so He is deeply concerned about justice. Listen to God speak through Isaiah regarding His desire for justice.

> For our transgressions are multiplied before you, and our sins testify against us; for our transgressions are with us, and we know our iniquities: transgressing, and denying the Lord, and turning back from following our God, speaking oppression and revolt, conceiving and uttering from the heart lying words. Justice is turned back, and righteousness stands far away; for truth has stumbled in the public squares, and uprightness cannot enter. Truth is lacking, and he who departs from evil makes himself a prey.
> (Isaiah 59:12-15)

Does this sound like any society with which

you might be familiar? Yes, sadly, we could write "America" in the margin next to these verses. But does God blame society? Does God speak words of challenge to the evil people because they do evil? Of course, God hates evil, and He will judge the evil, but notice what He says. "The Lord saw it, and it displeased him that there was no justice (Isa. 59:15). God was upset when justice was not done in the cities and the towns and the villages. God hates injustice. But notice further, "He saw that there was no man, and wondered that there was no one to intercede…" (Isa. 59:16).

God is revealing to us what grieves Him so deeply. It's not just evil, or injustice, or lying, but the tragedy that there was "no man" willing to step in and speak to this darkness, to pray about this, to call people to righteousness, and also to call upon God for mercy. God laments in these verses that there was no one willing to intercede.

God is deeply concerned about injustice, yet how often do we pray about wrongdoing? How often is the sin of injustice on our hearts to the extent that we pray about it? Are we willing to be instruments for justice? God says,

> Learn to do good; seek justice,
> correct oppression; bring justice to
> the fatherless, plead the widow's
> cause. (Isaiah 1:17)

Does this sound like God wants us to simply stand by and watch the world go down in the whirlpool of iniquity? No. God wants us to step forward and be people who seek justice. He wants us to help the oppressed and to defend the cause of those who are without defenders. He wants us to fight for those who have no one to help them—widows and orphans.

> "Thus says the Lord of hosts, Render [execute] true judgments, show kindness and mercy to one another, do not oppress the widow, the fatherless, the sojourner, or the poor, and let none of you devise evil against another in your heart." (Zechariah 7:9-10)

These are the concerns that are on God's heart. He has inscribed them in His Word to guide His people on their earthly mission for Him. God is a father to the fatherless and a husband to the widow.

So, who is on God's heart? Widows, the husbandless, orphans, the fatherless, aliens, the homeless, those who are far from their homeland, these are all on God's heart. They should be on our hearts as well and in our prayers.

As representatives of the King, we must remember how essential it is that we speak to

Him before we speak *for* Him. Our Master will give us guidance from His Word and by His Spirit about what we should say, and just as importantly, about how we should say it. His desire is that we always "speak the truth in love" (Eph. 4:15). Through prayer, He will give us the wisdom and courage to "say what He says," and He will also give us the humility and grace to say it in the right way. As He walked on the earth, our Lord was known as one "full of grace and truth," and it is through kneeling before Him in prayer that we are able to stand for the truth and to do so with a spirit of grace.

The causes of God—justice, mercy, and the message of salvation—is God's cause. He has on His heart the *salvation of the nations*. In Isaiah 49:6, God speaks through the prophet, Isaiah, to His Son, Jesus. What an awesome privilege it is when we get to listen to the Father talking to the Son.

> "It is too light a thing that you should be my servant to raise up the tribes of Jacob and to bring back the preserved of Israel; I will make you as a light for the nations, that my salvation may reach to the end of the earth." (Isaiah 49:6)

God says to His beloved Son, "I am so delighting in you that it is not enough that you are the Messiah to the Jewish people. You will be the light of My salvation to the ends of the earth." When we pray for missionaries and bring specific requests regarding their endeavors for evangelism before the Lord, we are participating in *their mission* and *His mission*.

Our specific requests should also include the salvation of our own people and loved ones. Paul shared about his specific request in Romans, Chapter 10, verse 1:

> Brothers, my heart's desire and prayer to God for them is that they may be saved.

Paul longed for his people to come to the Lord, so he prayed for their salvation. Lost people are God's great cause. Do we pray for them? *Our* personal salvation is God's great cause. As we talk about the topic of specific requests, we need to examine *our own hearts*. Can you say through Jesus Christ, and personal faith in Him, that God is your Heavenly Father?

As I write, I recall the story of my dear friend David and his guest that he brought to church recently. God spoke to his guest's heart, and he freely gave his life to Jesus. The first week David's guest attended, he did not know God as his Heavenly Father, and the next week he accepted Christ. Now he knows, without a doubt, that God is his Heavenly Father, and Christ is his Savior. One thing is certain: this man was on David's heart and in David's prayers long before he came into our church building. David had long been praying for his friend to come to know Jesus.

We should ask ourselves, "Do my prayer requests reflect God's causes? Do I pray about the kinds of things that are on God's heart? Do I need to re-order the priorities with His priorities? Do I ask these things in faith? Do I keep on asking, seeking, and knocking?"

It would be good to take a moment now and open our hearts to the Lord in prayer. Consider first what God has on His heart, and then reflect on what is on our heart. Remember always that we can be specific. *God will help us pray.*

> Likewise the Spirit helps us in our weakness. For we do not know what to pray for as we ought, but the Spirit himself intercedes for us with groanings too deep for words. And he who searches hearts knows what is the mind of the Spirit, because the Spirit intercedes for the saints according to the will of God.
> (Romans 8:26-27)

SPECIFIC REQUESTS

P
R
I
S

MEDITATION

5

OVER THE PREVIOUS CHAPTERS, WE'VE USED the acrostic *PRISM* as a reminder and guide to include various prayers in our times of devotion with the Lord. Of course, spending time with our Savior is a blessing, regardless of how time is structured. In fact, it is always best to allow the Lord to lead in any conversations we have with him! After all, he is the Master, and we are His followers. However, the Lord guides us in His Word regarding how He desires us to approach Him in prayer.

As we have mentioned previously, above all, prayer is a means of *praising* God. Prayer also involves *repentance*, as we acknowledge our sin and turn to God for forgiveness and restoration. Prayer should also involve *intercession,* when we kneel down to stand up for others as we bring their needs before Him.

We also shared in the previous chapter, the prayer focus of *specific requests*. When we pray, we need to make sure that our prayers are not just generalized "blessings," but that they include specific requests to our Heavenly Father who delights in hearing us bring our requests to Him.

In this chapter, we want to address a final and vitally important aspect of prayer—*meditation*. Surprisingly, many believers do not recognize this spiritual discipline as an expression of prayer, but it truly is. Meditation needs to be an integral part of our seasons of prayer to God. Meditation responds to the blessed reality that, as God's children, we are able to hear His voice. Prayer is more than just talking to God; it is a conversation *with* God. Prayer is so much more than just speaking words; it is worship. In times of prayer, God communicates with us, and we can hear *His* voice.

A beautiful example of this discernment of the Lord's voice is shared with us from a story in the life of the great prophet, Samuel. When Samuel was just a little boy, he lived in the tabernacle of God and was raised by Eli, the high priest. One quiet night in the Tent of Meeting, the Lord spoke to Samuel. At first, the young boy thought it was Eli calling him, so Samuel ran to his bedside and asked what he wanted him to do. Finally, Eli recognized that it was the Lord speaking to the boy, and he instructed Samuel to respond this way: "Speak Lord, your servant is listening" (1 Sam. 3:9). God gave a message to this little boy who was waiting in His presence, and Samuel was able to share God's message with others.

We learn from this passage in 1 Samuel, Chapter 3, a great deal about meditation. Inherent in this encounter between Samuel and the Lord is the truth that God speaks, and His message can be personally perceived. Meditation is a form of prayer in which we have mutual communication with God. God speaks to us, and we respond by speaking to God.

The basis of meditation is found in the nature of prayer itself. You see, above all things, prayer is communication, but not just one-way communication. Prayer is an interaction between us and God. It is essential to our understanding of prayer and our personal experience of prayer's fullness, that we recognize prayer as personal communication. Prayer is a mutual sharing—from the Father to us and then from us to the Father. Meditation is based on the incredible promise and living reality that we can communicate with God, and God will communicate with us.

It should not seem strange that God communicates to us personally because it is in the very nature of God to do so. God is self-revelatory, meaning that although He is so infinitely beyond our ability to comprehend, yet in His great love, He has chosen to reveal Himself to weak and sinful human beings. By choice, our God desires to reveal Himself and make Himself known. He is a God who speaks.

One of the titles that God uses to define and describe Himself is "The Word." The term "Word" itself communicates the idea that God is a speaking God. *He wants to be heard so that He can be known.* In fact, He promises to reveal Himself to those who sincerely want to know Him personally and walk with Him through life.

Since God is the "God Who Speaks," we need to remember that as we go to Him in prayer He is not silent. God is speaking. He speaks through all His creation around us. He speaks through His Word. He speaks to us by His Spirit to our spirit. The practice of Biblical meditation is a faith response to the conviction that our God desires to communicate with us personally. Of course, the most straightforward way that God has spoken to us is through the Incarnate Word of His Son, Jesus Christ.

The Apostle John tells us that no one has actually seen God at any time. God is invisible. However, the invisible God has become visible to us in Jesus. He is the Word made flesh, who has lived among us, so that we can, through Him, behold the glory of God (John 1:14,18). Likewise, we are told by the writer of Hebrews that God has spoken to us in these last days through His Son (Heb. 1:1). The writer of that epistle also tells us that this same God, who has spoken through the *Incarnate Word* of His Son, has also spoken to us through the *inspired Word* of His Book—the Bible. It is a Word, unlike any other.

> For the word of God is living and active, sharper than any two-edged sword, piercing to the division of soul and of spirit, of joints and of marrow, and discerning the thoughts and intentions of the heart. (Hebrews 4:12)

What a revelation we have in this verse about the Word of God! The Word of God is alive because it is alive with God's Spirit. The Spirit has given life to the words of Scripture. So, the words are *living words*; not dead words. We can genuinely say that the Bible is the voice of God. And we need to remember that God's voice is always *present tense* because He is the *present-tense God*.

> God is our refuge and strength, a **very present help** in trouble. Therefore we will not fear though the earth gives way, though the mountains be moved into the heart of the sea, though its waters roar and

foam, though the mountains tremble
at its swelling. Selah (Psalm 46:1-3)

The Bible is not a record of something God
said long, long ago. The Bible is a communication of what God is saying today, now.
Peter tells us that we are born again by "the
living and abiding word of God" (1 Pet. 1:23).
God is the eternal God. He is the ever-present
God. Therefore, when He speaks, He is
speaking in the *present-tense*. This is what
makes the concept of meditation so powerful. It
reminds us of what a tremendous privilege it is
for us, as believers, to know that our Heavenly
Father is speaking. And we, His children, can
hear His voice and understand the specific and
personal message He is sharing.

Because this is true, it is vitally important
that each of us knows how to meditate in
prayer-filled worship so that we can hear and
respond to the voice of our Heavenly Father.

THE FOUR "GETS"
OF MEDITATION

The basis of meditation rests in the fact
that God is a speaking God, and we are able to
hear His voice. But how do we specifically
practice listening to the Lord, which is so
essential to meditation? Many people have said
to me over the years, "Sam, I believe in

meditation, but I have to be honest. I don't get it." I have often responded to those people, "Well, I want to help you." Then I say, "Just forget it." They look at me inquisitively. And I repeat by saying, "Forget it."

Then they say something like this, "I don't understand, Sam. I thought you wanted to help me know how to practice meditation?" Then, *I spell it out* for them in a way I hope will help them and you *remember*—"FOUR Get It." Meaning, that there are "4 Gets" to meditation.

1. Get Serious In Determination

I recently read an article that described how a large number of people drove hours and camped out for several days for a chance to get tickets to attend a concert performed by a very famous entertainer. That willingness to sacrifice so much time, waiting for days, only to obtain the tickets to hear an entertainer is amazing.

Just imagine if we had that same kind of desire and determination to hear from God. What voice could possibly move or illuminate our minds as much as the voice of our Heavenly Father? And we can hear His voice. Our Father's voice is not silent, but He cannot be heard by those who are not sincerely committed to responding.

We have got to *get serious in determination*—serious like King David, who expressed his passion for hearing from the Lord this way:

> As a deer pants for flowing streams,
>   so pants my soul for you, O God.
> My soul thirsts for God,
>   for the living God.
> When shall I come and appear before God?
> My tears have been my food
>   day and night,
> while they say to me all the day long,
>   "Where is your God?"
>   (Psalm 42:1-3)

In this verse of song, we hear the hungry and thirsty heart of someone who is seeking God, who is *serious in determination*, and who is sincerely *hungry* for the Lord. Yes, the Lord will speak, He will communicate, but He only does so to those who are serious about their time with Him. We have to *get serious in determination* if we want to engage in Biblical meditation.

2. Get Close in Fellowship

Imagine right now, as you are reading this page, that I am going to reveal to you where ten million dollars is buried. Imagine also that there is a problem with my voice. I can only speak in a whisper. I am quite sure you would lean close, very close, and listen intently so that you could hear my directions to that buried treasure. Likewise, when God shares His precious Word with us, He usually speaks in a whisper. We want Him to shout. We want Him to speak very loudly because the world is noisy, and we want Him to speak very quickly, because well, we are very busy. But, that's not usually the way the Lord communicates to His children. The Heavenly Father does not shout at His kids. He speaks softly to His beloved children, and we hear His voice when we draw near to Him.

The Apostle James challenged us to close the distance between ourselves and our Father.

> Draw near to God, and he will draw
> near to you. (James 4:8a)

We draw near to God through worship. We can personally come before His holy presence. Even if we have wandered away, we are invited to return, and we are invited with a promise, "Draw near to God, and he will draw near to you." Think about this—God would not tell us to draw near to Him if He did not *want* to speak with us. The purpose of His invitation to come to Him is for personal fellowship, a fellowship that includes His desire to be heard and understood. Our Heavenly Father wants us to draw near. He wants to spend time with us. He desires us to fellowship with Him. He has not issued us a Judge's summons, but a Father's invitation. He invites us into a personal conversation. Amazing!

So, what does meditation require? Meditation requires for us to *get serious in determination*, to *get close in fellowship*, and then thirdly, to *get full of God's Word*. Meditation requires focusing our mind on the Word of God.

3. Get Full of God's Word

I love what David says regarding the truly "blessed person" in Psalm 1:1-2:

> Blessed is the man who walks not in
> the counsel of the wicked, nor stands
> in the way of sinners, nor sits in the
> seat of scoffers; but his delight is in
> the law of the Lord, and on his law
> he meditates day and night.

David connects the life of the blessed person with the practice of meditation. He describes the blessed person as one who meditates on God's law, day and night. We need to be clear. What does the word "meditation" mean? The word that David uses here has the idea of "murmur" or to "mutter." It is the idea of speaking to yourself, in particular, speaking back to yourself what God has shared in His Word. Meditation is speaking God's Word to yourself before you ever speak them to someone else. Meditation is focusing our minds on the *personal application* of the Word of God.

We often think of meditation today as putting our minds in a place of "void," removing all specific and personal thoughts from our minds. But that is entirely opposite to Biblical meditation. We only meditate when we *focus* our minds on God's Word and actually talk it back to ourselves. We *murmur* it to ourselves. We *mutter* it to ourselves. Meditation, in effect, is "self-talk" prompted by "God-talk."

David goes on to tell us about the wonderful results of meditation. He promises that any man or woman who will genuinely practice meditation on God's Word is guaranteed to be fruitful in life and find true success. However, meditation involves much more than just a "speed reading" of the Scripture. We must spend committed time in the Book. I often tell people that the key to our Christian life is Facebook—getting our face in the Book. We must read the Word, and more importantly, we need to let the Word *read us*. An enlightened mind results from an engaged mind that focuses, personally, on hearing and applying God's Word.

One of the reasons I strongly encourage people to read the Bible before their prayer time is to focus their mind on God's Word. By doing that, prayer becomes a response to God. God speaks to us from His Word, we consider what He says, we talk it over in our hearts and minds, and then we talk it back to Him in prayer. Prayer is a personal conversation with our Heavenly Father. We speak to God about what He has said to us. This is the wonderful experience of meditation, and it leads us, very naturally, into prayer.

When reading the Word becomes a process of careful consideration, when we apply His Word to our heart and then talk it back to God, our devotion time is transformed. Then, we are not just reading our Bibles; we are spending time with our Lord and holding a personal conversation with Him!

Meditation requires that we *get serious in determination*, we *get close in fellowship*, we *get full of God's Word*, and then fourthly, that we *get quiet in his presence*.

4. Get Quiet in His Presence

Prayer is talking to God. And just as importantly, prayer is also *listening* to God. Again, I love the insights that David, "a man after God's own heart," tells us about meditation and quietness before God.

> "Be still, and know that I am God. I
> will be exalted among the nations, I
> will be exalted in the earth!"
> (Psalm 46:10)

This is David sharing with us what he has heard from the Lord. "Be still and know that I am God." Those two qualities go together, inseparably. "*Being still*" and "*knowing God*."

When we are quiet in God's presence, we can discern His voice. We can't just rush through the Bible and then rush through prayer, just before we rush out the door, and expect that we are going to clearly hear God's voice in a profound and personal way. God is not in a hurry, and He will not allow us to rush or hurry Him. He loves us too much to do that.

We develop close friendships with those people with whom we share unhurried, personal conversations. It is the same in developing a close relationship with our greatest Friend. We need to stop rushing our relationship and begin sitting and being quiet with Him, listening to Him as He quietly speaks and then speaking to Him in return. We need to do exactly what that little boy Samuel did—be still, listen for our Master's voice, and at the first whisper from Him, respond, "Speak Lord. Your servant is listening."

As we begin to hear the Lord's voice, three responses are vitally important in the process of meditation.

THINK IT THROUGH

Before you begin to speak:

1. Think through what the Lord is sharing with you through His Word.
2. Carefully consider what you are sensing from Him as you are in His presence.
3. Make sure that you are not imposing your own thoughts onto Him but that the Word of God is guiding you as you turn the Scriptures over in your mind.
4. Remember, meditation is always our response to God's Word, not just our impressions.
5. Carefully consider the passage or passages you have read in their context.

The Bible has many applications, but only one interpretation. The words on the page mean something, and we must let them say what they mean. Prayerfully think through what the passage means. Use the help of a Study Bible, but most all, ask the Author for His help in understanding His Book.

TALK IT OUT

As you consider what the Word of God is saying, respond to the application that comes to your own heart by the prompting of the Holy Spirit. From what the Lord is saying to you, form a response back to Him. Maybe it will be a response of praise, repentance, intercession, or a specific request. In this way, meditation is completing the beautiful spectrum of PRISM. What the Lord is sending to you in His Word, you are returning to Him in your words. It is a personal, spiritual, and intimate conversation with your Master and Friend. Meditation becomes the oxygen of your prayer time, breathing life into those moments of communion, a conversation of Spirit to spirit. Meditation is the key to the PRISM of prayer—praise, repentance, intercession, specific requests—in response to God's Spirit, speaking to our hearts.

WRITE IT DOWN

Think it through, talk it out, and then *write it down.* I encourage you to have your times of devotion with a pen and notebook at hand. As you hear God speaking to you, and as you sense Him leading you into praise, or repentance or intercession, or specific requests, interpret this as the Lord's communication to you. An incredibly effective way of assisting in meditation is to write down the insights and impressions that come to you in times of personal worship and devotion. Journaling the things that God is giving to you during your time of devotion, engages your mind with a clear focus, and the result becomes a written or typed record of your spiritual journey with the Lord.

You will find that returning to those pages helps you recognize that the Holy Spirit is truly writing a "living epistle" in you and through you (2 Cor. 2:3). I cannot begin to share what a blessing it has been for me to take some of the journals from past years, open them up, and read how the Lord ministered to my heart during the various seasons of my life's journey with Him. Reading those journals from many, many years ago, gives me a very present and living message from God's heart to mine. It encourages me that the Lord has always been speaking to me, He is speaking to me today, and He will continue to reveal Himself to me as I seek Him.

*   *   *

Few things are as beautiful as the colors of the spectral light—the colors of the rainbow. In a very special way, that is what our times of prayer can be—a PRISM of worship, a beautiful, multi-colored, and glorious encounter with the covenant-keeping God.

My friend, as we come to our conclusion on the subject of prayer, my prayer is that you will experience God through your times in prayer that is full of *Praise, Repentance, Intercession, Specific Requests,* and *Meditation.* May you encounter, over and over again, our beautiful, living Lord. He invites you to come boldly before His throne. It is a throne of grace, and above it shines—today and throughout the endless ages to come—a rainbow.

Amen.

MEDITATION

Prayer Photo Recognition

Praise: Nathan Dumlao
Repentance: KTMD ENTERTAINMENT
Intercession: Jon Tyson
Specific Requests: Nathan Dumlao
Meditation: Fa Barboza on Unsplash

SAM POLSON is the Lead Pastor of West Park Baptist Church in Knoxville, Tennessee, and featured teacher with the SonLight Radio media ministry. He also currently serves as Chairman of the Board for ABWE, the Association of Baptists for World Evangelism, and previously served for many years on the Board of Shepherds Ministries, an educational ministry for adults with developmental disabilities. Sam was born and raised in New Castle, Indiana, where he met and married his wife, Susan. He earned his Bachelor's and Master's degree in theology from Bob Jones University and then served seven years as an assistant pastor at Calvary Baptist Church in Findlay, Ohio. The Polsons then moved to Knoxville, where Sam has served as Lead Pastor for more than 34 years. They have three grown children who live in the Knoxville area. Sam advises the pastoral team and staff, teaches in large and small group settings, and is the most energized by witnessing people come alive to the reality of the gospel. Sam Polson's other books include *In His Image, By Faith, SonLight* (a daily devotional), and *Corona Victus: Conquering the Virus of Fear*.

"For what we proclaim is not ourselves, but Jesus Christ as Lord, with ourselves as your servants for Jesus' sake" (2 Corinthians 4:5).

ABOUT CLIMBING ANGEL
PUBLISHING

Climbing Angel Publishing exists for the purpose of sharing stories of hope and encouragement, aiding in the gathering together of community, and supporting the process of betterment. The following books are available at ClimbingAngel.com and major bookstores.

Adult Books: *(Romans 8:28-30)*

In His Image
By Faith
My Birthday Gift to Jesus
Without Ceasing
SonLight
Corona Victus: Conquering the Virus of Fear
Art Bushing: His Diary, Letters, &
Photographs of WWII
Art & Dotty: His Diary, Their Letters &
Photographs of WWII
Trimisul, Stan Johnson (Romanian)
Life Changing Prayer

Children's Books: *(Philippians 4:8)*

The Christmas Tree Angel
The Unmade Moose
Thump
Somebunny To Love
The Truth About God's Rainbow
God's Promises
The Boy & The Bagel Necklace
I Like To Be Quiet
Wheels Off!

CPSIA information can be obtained
at www.ICGtesting.com
Printed in the USA
LVHW041332221120
672366LV00002B/2